Seriously,
Life Is a Laughing
Matter

Seriously, Life Is a Laughing Matter

Tom Mullen

WORD BOOKS
PUBLISHER
WACO, TEXAS

SERIOUSLY, LIFE IS A LAUGHING MATTER
Copyright © 1978 by Word Incorporated

Quotation at beginning of chapter 16 is from "The Death of the Hired Man" from *The Poetry of Robert Frost* edited by Edward Connery Lathem. Copyright 1930, 1939, © 1969 by Holt, Rinehart and Winston. Copyright © 1958 by Robert Frost. Copyright © 1967 by Lesley Frost Ballantine. Reprinted by permission of Holt, Rinehart and Winston, Publishers.

ISBN 0-8499-0073-5
Library of Congress catalog card number: 77-92451
Printed in the United States of America

To Ivan and Susan Cooper

Contents

Preface 9
1. A Light-hearted Call to a Devout and Holy Life 13
2. The Curse of the Conscientious 17
3. Garage Sales and the Meaning of Life 21
4. "Cool" Is Not So Hot 25
5. The Bottom Line 29
6. I'm Not O.K. and You're Not Perfect, Either 33
7. Work Is a Four-Letter Word 37
8. On Putting First Things First 41
9. On Self-Denial and Other Excesses 45
10. Unhappy Are the Hard-Boiled 49
11. Irresistible Forces and Immovable Objects 53
12. Joyful Noises Slightly Off-Key 57
13. Up Close, I'm Something Special 61
14. Too Much Civilization 65
15. Hurrah for Amateurs! 69
16. Keeping Up with Upkeep 73
17. We Are Where We Eat 77
18. Heroes and Heroines 81
19. In Praise of "Old" Lovers 85
20. The Lord Loves a Cheerful Crusader 89
21. Living Can Be Hazardous to Your Health 93
22. Why the Reaper Is Grim 97

Preface

There are Deep Meanings in most fairy tales which, if brought out by parents at bedtime, will cause their children to fall asleep faster. *The Three Bears* is a case in point.

You'll recall that Goldilocks, upon realizing that she was trespassing, complicated her crime by vandalism. The porridge was too hot or too cold, but one bowl was Just Right, so she ate it all up. Two chairs didn't fit, but a third was Just Right and Goldilocks sat on it and broke out the bottom. One bed was too hard, another was too soft, but a third one was Just Right.

The Deeper Meaning is that we, like Goldilocks, have to experiment with life before we discover what is Just Right for us. If we believe there's lots in life to enjoy—far more than we've been led to think—we're still left with the adventure of finding out how seriously to take it.

Thus, this book is about when to laugh and how heartily. It also touches, necessarily, on laughter's counterpart: when to take life seriously. Much of the book is based on personal adventures within the author's family and observations made while allegedly working as a teacher at Earlham School of Religion. Other chapters reflect on Life in General and how it gets bruised when taken too seriously.

I discovered while writing that the line between tragedy and comedy, tears and laughter, is not clearly drawn. We experience both in finding what is Just Right. Irvin S. Cobb said, "Humor is merely tragedy standing on its head with its pants down." I would add that life taken too seriously is like swimming while wearing a tuxedo. It's too formal a response to an unpredictable situation.

My hope is that this book will encourage its readers to risk light-heartedness more often. 'Tis better to laugh at the wrong times than never to laugh at all. Our lives, as Emerson reminds us, are not apologies. They are lives. They will necessarily be *full of* apologies, but they are to be taken seriously because life is a gift from God. They can be lived with good humor for the same reason.

Material in some of the chapters appeared previously in "Mullin' It Over," a monthly column in *The Disciple*. I am grateful to James Merrell, its editor, for risking the dignity of his magazine by publishing such material.

Thanks, also, to Doris Burkhart, Peggy Estes, and Claudia Ettel for typing the manuscript. Getting it completed under severe time limitations was no small task, particularly when arrows, insertions, and microscopic additions made the job an adventure.

Nancy, whose ability to laugh at her husband's humor goes beyond duty to the point of sacrifice, merits deep appreciation and some blame. Parts of this book are mushy and sentimental, and the fault is hers because she continues to inspire romantic feelings after more than twenty years of marriage.

Sarah, our college-student daughter, insisted upon censorship rights over any material involving her. As a result most of the embarrassing family incidents reported herein are about her sisters, Martha and Ruthie, and her brother, Bret.

The book is dedicated to Ivan and Sue Cooper. Suzy came to live with us when she was sixteen and, as she put it, "unfortunately, they always treated me as one of the family." She had the good sense to marry Ivan, however, and together they have managed to combine hard work and happy dispositions in a way that is Just Right. I confess having enormous pride in them, so much that it borders on sinfulness. Since my chromosomes deserve no credit for their achievements, however, I assume I'm forgiven and dedicate this volume to them with love and one free copy.

Tom Mullen

I

A Light-hearted
Call to a Devout
and Holy Life

Consider the following stories, which can be told publicly at a church meeting:

>—A young boy, upon returning home from his first circus, comments: "Once you've been to a circus, you'll never enjoy prayer meeting again!"

>—A mountaineer, after he had returned from Europe following World War I, remarked: "I shore wisht I'd seen Paris before I was converted."

>—A temperance speaker became carried away by his own rhetoric: "Why, dear friends, I would rather commit adultery than take a drink!" An anonymous voice from the audience responded, "So would I."

Such stories, clean enough to tell in public and old enough to be familiar to several generations, share a common characteristic. They all suggest that practicing the Christian faith is less enjoyable than the alternatives. They imply that religion is like going to the dentist; if it is good for us, it is supposed to hurt.

Take, for example, the connotation of the word *puritan.* "Puritanism" represents stern obedience, God peeking over our shoulder, and dark judgment of our sins. H. L. Mencken said that it is "the haunting fear that someone, somewhere is having a good time." And often, at least in the secular mind, "puritan" is equated with "Christian."

Unfortunately, this sour reputation is deserved—at least in part. All of us know Christians who have taken themselves so seriously they have spoiled the message. We know mothers and fathers who worry constantly over their children, transforming motherhood into smotherhood. There are teetotalers who drive us to drink, pacifists who make us want to fight, and superpatriots who are living arguments for defecting. When righteousness becomes self-righteousness, the result is something other than Jesus intended.

Persons trying to be Christian are not the only ones tempted to take life too seriously. Scratch a hedonist, and a "natirup" (that's a puritan in reverse) will be found. Cynics are hard-boiled eggs who are so tough they never let life hurt them—or touch them, either. The blasé never worry over their sins and consequently miss out on all the blood-boiling, sinus-clearing effects of old-fashioned moral indignation. Pagans taking paganism too seriously don't have any more fun than Puritans do—if we count the time spent drying out from the night before.

Life, after all, is very serious, but it's not all *that* serious. A key to abundant living is knowing when and how to treat it seriously and when and how to roll with its punches. Such knowledge is high, and we do not always attain it. At times we've laughed when we should've kept quiet or moralized when we'd have done better to enjoy a private joke in our minds.

Still, the principle is sound: *laugh whenever we can*. Laughing at ourselves will protect us from false piety, self-righteousness, and pontificating. A serious call to a devout and holy life needs some tongue in its cheek to insure both sanity and humility. The Christian life has always needed a comic perspective, and those able to laugh at the foibles of self and others are twice blessed.

Fortunately, we have some excellent examples of persons who have managed to take life seriously while recognizing that it is a laughing matter. Some examples, in fact, are ancient; some people discovered how to do this long before this book was written. The following, allegedly the prayer of a 17th century nun, is a case in point.

O Lord, keep me from getting talkative.
And particularly from the fatal habit that I must say something on every subject and on every occasion.

Release me from the craving to straighten out everybody's affairs.

Keep my mind free from the recital of endless details; give me wings to get to the point. Seal my lips when inclined to tell of my aches and pains.

They are increasing with the years and my love of rehearsing them grows sweeter as the years go by.

Teach me the glorious lesson that occasionally it is possible that I may be mistaken.

Keep me reasonably sweet. I do not want to be a Saint. Some of them are hard to live with, but a sour old woman is one of the crowning works of the devil.

Help me to extract all possible fun out of life. There are
so many funny things around us, and I do not want to
miss any of them.

Make me thoughtful but not moody, helpful but not
bossy.

With my vast store of wisdom it seems a pity not to use
it all, but Thou, my Lord, knoweth that I want a few
friends left at the end.

Her words are more than a prayer. They demonstrate a perspective about life which is Christian in
and of itself. It is a viewpoint which sees around and
over the log in one's own eye. It hates sins but loves
sinners. It is a light-hearted call to a devout and holy
life.

2
The Curse of the Conscientious

Conscientious Christians believe in Murphy's Law. They have good reason to do so, as Murphy's anonymous insights have proven remarkably accurate since first articulated. No one knows for sure who Murphy was, although some researchers are convinced she was a retired female blackmailer born and raised in Salt Lake City around the turn of the century.

Nevertheless, her—or his—first law must be considered whenever we discuss the meaning of life. That law, as millions know, is: *if anything can go wrong, it will.*

Applied to human experience, the relevance of Murphy's insight is obvious. For example, we may resolve, with teeth-gritting determination, to save money. The Bible warns us against storing resources, of course, but the conscientious Christian is sustained by John Wesley who urged us to earn all we can, save all we can, and give away all we can. Saving money, therefore, is a worthy goal, but it fails to take seriously the Murphy-derived truth that *everything you decide to do costs more than first estimated.* Thus, not only do we fail to save money; we also end up spending more than planned. Consequently, we fall victim to the Biblical warning that there will be "great gnashing of teeth in the land," not to mention extra trips to the dentist to repair gnashed molars.

What are we to do, those of us who are reasonably willful, moderately disciplined, and somewhat conscientious, in the face of Murphy and her (or his) sadly discouraging laws? In whatever we attempt, we will probably discover that *something else must be done first.*

Did you carefully organize your committee and get them to the church on time? You should have picked up the key to the building first. You've invited a prominent and expensive speaker to give a life-changing address to all who hear? Next time check the bowling league schedule, as it ranks before changing lives.

Ask the chairperson of any church committee, and each will agree that *every activity takes more time than there is available to perform it.* Set aside two hours for a one-hour task, and your committee will decide to accomplish more than it originally intended —which will take more time than you have available. Which means more meetings. Murphy strikes again!

Such are the workings of Murphy's Laws, and—like gravity—they have much to do with the ups and downs of life (pun intended). There is considerable evidence to support Murphy's contention that *nothing is ever as simple as it first seems,* and any of us who has ever attacked a leaky faucet has learned experientially the Murphyism, *if we tinker with something long enough, eventually it will break.* Even you, faithful reader, may be realizing as you struggle with this chapter that *any effort to make something absolutely clear will confuse people!*

The question remains: what are we to do? The answer is that we need to set gospel alongside law, even Murphy's, to get a complete picture of the human condition. Yes indeed, life is a fumbled punt, and every day we fall back to receive another kick. Fortunately, it is more than that, especially when we add the good news that we are accepted by the Grace of God, booboos and all.

One redeemed realist put it this way: "I'm not O.K. You're not O.K. And that's O.K!" The curse of conscientious Christians is the nagging feeling they are not quite acceptable unless they measure up. They need to know that God's grace is available to all. Even now, as they strain, strive, and struggle, they have gifts to give and a place in God's kingdom.

Please don't misunderstand. The world needs obsessive compulsives—airplane pilots who triple-check the controls, surgeons who count their instruments after an operation, and accountants who demand receipts for everything purchased and sold in this world and the next. Loosey-goosey Larry can enjoy the luxury of his loosi-goosiness when he flies in a plane or has his appendix removed or is audited by the IRS—if Uptight Terry has been on the job.

Murphy is right in her (or his) analysis. She (or he) just doesn't go far enough. Yes, things will go wrong, but being conscientious isn't the trouble. The problem is in knowing we're acceptable, blocked punts and all. Once that news is internalized, a genuine miracle occurs. An obsessive compulsive relaxes—right after checking the chair for structural defects.

3
Garage Sales and the Meaning of Life

Let it be hereby reported that private enterprise is alive and well in the United States. While the stock market may sputter and Wall Street gasp, though warehouses groan with an overstock of goods in search of buyers, the most important of our capitalistic institutions continues to thrive and prosper.

We refer, of course, to middle-class America's boutique—the garage sale. These backyard bazaars go by many names, such as tag sales, flea markets, or rummage sales. Yet, as a deservedly unknown poet has written:

> A garage sale by any other name
> Sells lots of junk that's all the same.

Garage sales have spawned their own breed of groupies—itinerant bargain hunters who devote entire weekends to traipsing from garage to garage in search of the "ultimate find." Indeed, what seems to dictate whether one *goes* to garage sales or *holds* them is to

decide which brings the greater pleasure—picking up
bargains or unloading a dud. It takes two, after all, to
make a bargain, but only one gets it. For better or
worse, the fact remains that one person's dud is another's priceless treasure, and on such Truth does the
garage sale depend.

Novices, either buyers or sellers, are astounded at
the mind-boggling variety of useless items at family
flea markets. "Who would be crazy enough to pay three
dollars for a rusty old coffee grinder?" a man may ex-
claim, shortly before buying an antique porch swing
for ten dollars, even though he doesn't have a porch.
His logic? If ever he adds a porch to his house, he'll
be prepared. Besides, he had a porch swing when he
was a boy.

Clothes are the stock in trade at nearly all rummage
sales, and many poor people consistently outfit their
families with good used clothing from such events.
Other customers come for different reasons, including
a few irate husbands searching for favorite hats or
jackets given to the church rummage sale by wives
trying to coerce them into buying new ones. Such even-
tualities invariably cause disharmony in the home,
since one of two hostility-producing responses is forth-
coming. Either the favorite jacket is sold, which, as
Joseph discovered in the Old Testament, demonstrates
rejection by one's family; or it is not sold for its fifty-
cent price, a serious blow to any man's estimate of his
sartorial taste.

Garage sales also become the regular beats of col-
lectors and those who want something for nearly
nothing, whether they be on a quest for ten-year old
clothes that have returned to style or mis-matched
china that matches their own. Some come looking for
antiques, items that are valuable less in terms of age

than definition. Antiques, after all, are merely fugitives from a garage sale with a price on their heads.

People who are able to buy the top line of the most expensive products will brag for days about an adorable little chair they bought for a dollar at a flea market. Others will admire their purchases for ten minutes after returning home and then relegate them to the attic—until they can unload them on some other gullible traveler to garage sales. Thus it is that old bargains never die; they are merely reincarnated in somebody else's carport.

What, patient readers, is the deeper meaning of the garage sale? Is it a metaphor for life?

In one way it is like a disorganized personality test in which we find out many frightening things about ourselves. We discover within ourselves greed, exploitative tendencies, and at least small doses of all seven deadly sins.

In another sense the garage sale is a testimony to the human spirit. It witnesses to the belief that someday we will get organized and unclutter our lives and maybe even rise above our need to acquire things in order to feel secure.

In short, it reveals us to be both good and bad, strong and weak, wise and foolish. Consequently, the garage sale will probably always be with us, or at least as long as our junk is where our heart is.

4

"Cool" Is
Not So Hot

Adults who are Christian are a lot like little children. True, they're bigger, usually more polite, and seldom spill their milk. Like children, however, they are almost never "cool."

Unfortunately, "cool" is in. "Cool" means not to get involved. It is to count the cost before acting. It is to practice cautious skepticism. Give a skeptic an inch, and he'll measure it. "Cool" people are calculating about life, and they check their emotional involvements very carefully.

Children, on the other hand, are impulsive. Their responses are spontaneous, and they quickly get involved with others. The adult world dampers their free spirits in several ways. Television and other exploiters rip off their minds so as to sell them toys and breakfast foods. Good parents, in response, teach their children caution so they won't get ripped off so much. Nevertheless, until their corruptors and their protectors succeed in making them "cool," kids are often childlike.

The language of Transactional Analysis recognizes this quality and identifies that part of the human per-

sonality which tends to spontaneity as "the child."
T.A. also says that maturity is knowing when to let
our "child" out in those moments when we can savor
and enjoy life.

"Cool" people lock their "child" inside. They dare
not laugh at corny jokes because to do so shows a lack
of sophistication. The trivial must be avoided at all
costs, for it reveals a lack of profundity. Childlike
students go to a record hop to dance, "cool" students
go to be seen *not* dancing, and faculty occasionally go
to make a sociological analysis of primordial impulses.
With Tallyrand, the "cool" of the world distrust first
impulses because they are almost always right.

The Apostle Paul was seldom "cool" about life. He
honored some because they were "noble," respected
others for their courage, and still others for their
loyalty. Yet Paul also saved a special adjective for
some comrades which is worth coveting for ourselves.
He described Stephanas, Fortunatus, and Achaicus as
"refreshing" (1 Cor. 16:18). Phillips' translation says
it best: "They are a tonic to me."

A childlike spirit is a tonic, a refresher. Spontaneous
words mean what they say. There is no trickery involved. It is refreshing when a child says to her
mother, "Wow, Mom, you look great!"—partly because
it happens so seldom.

Spontaneous remarks ask nothing in return. They
are not calculated to sell us anything. They do not ask
the question: what will people say? As a result they
both refresh us and sometimes get us in trouble. I remember with mixed pleasure and pain a boyhood comment which was clearly childlike, in that it was both
impulsive and trouble-causing.

I was attending Boys' State, where each living unit

underwent daily inspection by a military officer. Our quarters were to be immaculate, as were our persons. Unfortunately, a retired colonel made a surprise inspection of our unit, coming before I had shaved the few miserable whiskers my adolescent face had been able to produce.

I recall vividly his stopping directly in front of me while I stood rigidly at attention. He scrutinized me from bottom to top, finally focusing a frowning stare on my pitiful fuzz. Reaching out, he patted me under the chin. "What's the matter, son, don't you have a razor?"

Somewhere, from out of the tense silence, I heard my voice reply, "Yes, sir, but I don't loan it to strangers."

That remark, still fixed in my memory twenty-seven years later, brought me great satisfaction and guffaws of laughter from my friends. It also brought the maximum number of demerits allowed under Boys' State rules. Mischief can be the manure which nurtures a childlike spirit, demerits notwithstanding!

Astonishment, along with spontaneity and mischief, form the trinity of childlikeness. A. A. Milne, the author of the Pooh books, described a child's inheritance of wonder. He wrote of a boy's list of amazing things he could see while out for a walk: sun on a river and a hill, the sound of the sea "if you stand quite still," new puppies at a nearby farm, and—most awe-inspiring of all—an old sailor with an empty sleeve.

Adults too easily become a Society for the Suppression of Astonishment. Ours is a world glutted with fact, information, and entertainment but deficient in wonder. There is an unending parade of novelties, all of which can be explained by mechanics. The older we get, the less novelties seem novel. Life becomes stale, flat, and wearisome to many people because the wonder is left out.

Halford Luccock put it this way: "Life is truly measured not by the number of breaths taken, but by the number not taken, the occasions when breath is stopped in amazement." Such a standard knocks the ice cubes out of "cool," for if there is anything that astonishment is *not*, it is calculating or skeptical.

If we can keep our heads while all around us are losing theirs, says the pundit, it may be that we have not properly assessed the situation. He may be right. For if we can lose our heads—commit mischief and experience astonishment—while all around us are keeping theirs, we just may have properly assessed the situation. At least we will find refreshment for our souls and possibly, by the grace of God, be refreshing to others as well.

5

The Bottom Line

Children come off rather well in the New Testament. While Jesus was continually hassling the Pharisees and often giving his disciples a hard time for their thick-headedness, his few encounters with children are positive.

There are reasons for this. Not only was Jesus, after all, who he was, but, it also is important to note, he was a bachelor. He never had to put little kids to bed at night when they didn't want to go. He never had to get them to clean their rooms right after they and their friends had made Sherman's march to the sea look tidy by comparison. There is no New Testament record of his response to an eight-year-old boy who keeps feeding broccoli to the dog.

The King James translator, however, was undoubtedly a parent. Only a parent would have translated Mark 10:14: "*Suffer* the little children to come." Even though "suffer" didn't mean then what it means today, it should have. Children are not as innocent as their reputations would have us believe. In many ways they are like real people, exhibiting perversity and selfishness just like adults.

Even so, we are called to be "childlike" if we would enter the Kingdom. The question is: if we *already* share pride, jealousy, and nastiness with them, what special quality remains?

Surely Jesus means "innocence" in a certain sense. He must have meant the capacity of a child to ask the obvious question, to get to the heart of the matter, to cut through pretense and sham. As the familiar story of "The Emperor's New Clothes" shows, children will see the truth before adults because they are less trapped by rationalizations and subterfuge.

This writer's youngest child has demonstrated such a capacity again and again. Our vacationing family once visited Old Town in Chicago, a section of that city famous for its arts, crafts, and restaurants. In recent years, alas! it has also attracted pornographic movie houses and prostitutes who solicit customers openly on the streets. While such is the curse of cities where legitimate artists and crafts dealers gather, it had not been true on our previous visit there and so came as a surprise to the family.

Thus Ruthie, seven years old and curious, was fascinated by a set of sights and sounds different from what her parents had intended. "Why isn't that woman wearing any underwear, Mommy?" "Daddy, what does l-u-s-t mean?" "How come all those men are going into that place?"

Parents, who know what l-u-s-t means, nonetheless have difficulty explaining it to small children. In place of explanations, they attempt to distract, to get their children interested in something better for their minds and souls. So they ignore questions and call attention to the nice man blowing glass blobs into tiny animals.

Unfortunately, this particular child continued to be fascinated by the obviously female shapes dancing in neon lights on nearby marquees. Her Mother Goose books had neglected to provide such sights, and one nice man creating glass puppy dogs was no match.

The father, wise to the ways of the world, eventually confronted the persistent questioning of his child with honesty and forthrightness: "Go ask your mother, dear." The mother, resisting the temptation to grab the blow torch and re-shape her husband, finally laid it on the line: "Those men are buying tickets to see somebody's bare bottom."

Candor with children sometimes concludes a conversation, but not often—and not in this instance. "But," Ruthie asked, "why would anybody pay money to see somebody's bare bottom?"

Why, indeed? Why do we spend money for magazines, movies, television shows, and pictures based on sexual appeal? Adults will cloud a discussion of such issues with concerns for "freedom of expression" and "fears of censorship." What kind of man reads *Playboy?* Witty, sophisticated types who pay to see somebody's bare bottom. In fact, when we consider the commercial success of such magazines, our seven-year-old probably had given the basic explanation. She had identified the "bottom" line.

A child will want to know why some white people are so mean to black people. A history of the war between the states or a careful sociological analysis will not cause that question to disappear. A small child can ask a parent, "Daddy, why do people kill each other in wars?" and any answer will seem unsatisfactory because it can't be given without including its layers of hate and nationalism.

The adult inclination is to say, "You're too young to

understand, honey. Look at the nice man blowing glass in the window." Maybe so. Maybe, though, adults are too old to understand. A child-spirit is able to see the truth, and do it. Maturity means to grow up, but Jesus' point is that "growing up" should have a child-like perspective.

James Russell Lowell, when passing a building in the outskirts of Boston, noticed an identifying inscription: "Home for Incurable Children." To a friend he remarked, "They'll get me in there some day." That's a worthwhile wish for ourselves, too. If we would enter the Kingdom, that is exactly what we'll need to be —incurable children.

6
I'm Not O.K., and You're Not Perfect Either

The sneakiest of Jesus' parables is that of the Pharisee and the tax collector. The Pharisee, obviously, is a pious ass: "God, I thank thee, that I am not as other men are, extortioners, unjust, adulterers, or even as this publican. I fast twice in the week, I give tithes of that I possess" (Luke 18:11–12 KJV).

The tax collector, of course, is truly penitent in his prayer: "God be merciful to me a sinner." This is where it gets sneaky. We almost always say to ourselves, "Thank God I'm not like that Pharisee."

It is easy to caricature the Pharisee. We can draw him in broad strokes. He's a good example of a bad example. Not so with the tax collector. How does one show humility and, even harder, how does one emulate a penitent person? ("C'mon, gang, let's be like the tax collector. First, practice beating your breast. That's it, not too hard. Now glance down with the eyes—no, not straight down, more to the side and with the slightest flutter of the eyelids. By George, they've got it!")

Piety is always tricky. It has to do with humility and sincerity, prayer, and devotions. It comes recommended by all, but authentic piety is harder to grasp than a big bar of wet soap one-handed when your eyes are blinded by shampoo. The moment we think about our own piety, it slips away.

Public prayers provide never-ending examples of piety gone sour. Many are really little sermonettes given with eyes closed and head bowed. A few have been used to make announcements left out of the bulletin: "O Lord, Thou knowest the next time we meet will be at 7:00 in the church parlor." Or some of them are delivered in stained-glass vocabulary for the benefit of posterity: Protect us, O Beneficent Father, from vicissitudes and deprivations. . . ." (Editorial note: whatever *they* are!)

Private prayers are not always as holy as our postures and countenances suggest. Our minds wander, and it is easy to focus upon the immediate rather than the eternal. ("O Lord, grant that I did turn the oven down.") Even prayers for the sick are vulnerable to selfish interests: "Watch over Mrs. Burke, Lord, even though Thou knowest I had more gall stones than she did."

Piety is damaged, in other words, whenever we focus on how *we're* doing in the act of praying or serving. It is experienced authentically when we lose ourselves in the act and are not preoccupied with our performance. One meaning of the word "Pharisee," in fact, is "Separatist." Pharisees held themselves aloof. They made comparisons.

Herein lies the key. Wherever it occurs in the common adventures of life, it is the comparing—the calling attention to self—that transforms prayer into pronouncements, service into obligations, and witness into advertising. Third, second, and first person comparatives tease us with this truth:

She is a hypocrite, you are pious, I am devout.

He is sneaky, you are crafty, I am subtle.

She is hidebound, you are old-fashioned, I revere tradition.

His son is a bum, yours is a hippy, mine is trying to find himself.

She is snappy, you are contentious, I stand up for my rights.

He is childish, you are immature, I am young at heart.

She is slovenly, you are untidy, I like a house to have a nice lived-in look.

He is hen-pecked, you are anxious, I am married to a fine little woman whose opinions I respect.

Creating our own comparatives is a good spiritual discipline. They remind us with each writing about specks and logs in our eyes.

He has a log in his eye, you have a speck, I've left my contacts in too long.

It was Kierkegaard who said: "Prayer doesn't change God, but changes him who prays." He meant genuine prayer, no doubt, for any other kind feeds our self-satisfaction and leaves calcium deposits on the soul. Real prayer rounds off comparatives and puts us all in the same category: we are people who have fallen short. The old gospel song put it properly: "Not my brother, nor my sister, but it's me, O Lord, standin' in the need of prayer." To that he says, you say, and I say, "Amen."

7
Work Is a
Four-Letter Word

In the good old U.S. of A. excessive work is lauded, praised, expected, and frequently demanded. We have a holiday to honor labor. Many of us delight in telling how early we go to work or how late we stayed.

Some pastors have carried an inferiority complex because they've heard too often the shopworn comment, "Sure wish I had a job where I only had to work one day a week." Hence, clergypersons often put in more hours than anyone else on the block in order to justify their calling.

For better or worse, many of us cling to the Old Testament idea that failure is a sign of sin and success a sign of virtue. We work extra hard on extra jobs to earn extra money to buy things we don't need to impress people we don't like. At one time in our history when a person worked twelve hours per day, it was called economic slavery. Nowadays, it's called moonlighting, and many people hold two jobs so they can drive from one to the other in a more expensive car.

This is not to say that workaholics are evil. Not so. Corporations and many other institutions, to prosper as organizations, need a few persons who are obsessed with work. All work and no play may make Jack a dull boy, but to management he's the life of the party. No, the problem is essentially a religious one: we try to justify our existence by our work. Workaholics are kindred spirits with obsessive compulsives. More work means more justification.

Justification by work is a message delivered to our young people more often than we suppose. A dramatic example is seen in the following Associated Press release:

> Amy, 15, had always gotten straight A's in school, and her parents were extremely upset when she got a B on her report card. 'If I fail in what I do,' Amy told her parents, 'I fail in what I am.' The message was part of Amy's suicide note.

Amy is not alone. The number of teenage suicides in the United States has tripled in the last decade, to an estimated 30 per day. More than half the patients in the nation's psychiatric hospitals are under age twenty-one.

Undoubtedly, there are many reasons for this phenomenon, but among them, according to several psychologists, is the belief that the person who does or produces more is more important—the belief in justification by works.

Fortunately, there are people around who provide a corrective for this attitude. Many of them are children who have not yet caught the disease, who somehow feel justified without having to prove it. It was a small child who put it this way: "God made a lot of days so you wouldn't try to do every thing at once." *

---

* *God Is a Good Friend to Have* (New York: Simon and Schuster, 1969), p. 47.

Our only son, Bret, continually reminds his parents and sisters that work is not the beginning, middle, and end of life. Bret is aware that hard work never hurt anyone, but he clearly has a low threshhold of pain. Lecturettes given by father to son on this topic vary somewhat in content, but they have a common theme: "Work harder, son."

The following conversation, slightly edited for the religious market, is illustrative:

Dad: Bret, I want you to paint the carport. It needs painting and you'll learn the satisfaction that comes from working hard.

Bret: Why do I have to learn to work hard?

Dad: Well, if you learn to work hard, you'll be able to get and keep a good job when you grow up. Then, if you save your money, you can do what you want.

Bret: If I didn't have to paint, I'd be doing what I want now.

Higher criticism of the above passage reveals flaws in Bret's thinking; he is, after all, not taking seriously enough his dependence on others. Yet it also shows that there are things worse than to live without working. One of them is to *work without living*. Putting our hands to the grindstone is not the same as putting our noses there. Samuel Johnson said it best: "No man is obliged to do as much as he can do; a man has to have part of his life to himself."

The ancient Hebrews knew this instinctively. The Sabbath was set aside out of thanksgiving for deliverance from slavery. Or, stated positively, it expressed gratitude for freedom. The early Christians reserved the Lord's Day as a day of rest and gladness, and it was the *first* day of the week.

To work too hard, too long, or too much is to take work too seriously. For those of us who are borderline workaholics, we need to develop the capacity to do nothing. This is not an easy task. Just getting untangled from having our eye on the ball, our ear to the ground, and our shoulder to the wheel will take considerable effort.

Stated below, free of charge, is one formula that may help. It has four steps, but you can skip the first three if you like.

1. Take long walks in the woods, unless you'd rather not.
2. Read magazines in the bathroom.
3. Don't go anywhere on vacations.
4. Ignore the first three and "don't do" what you want.

Workaholics of the world, unite! We have nothing to lose but our guilt feelings, and those, dear friends, are worth losing.

8

On Putting
First Things First

When members of primitive societies beat the ground with clubs and yell, their actions are studied by anthropologists and called witchcraft. When this happens in twentieth-century America, we name it golf.

Indeed, for millions of Americans golf is like a religion, albeit a primitive one. Self-made executives who are masters of their fate and captains of their souls plead with deities to nudge a small ball into a slightly larger hole. These same supplicants, however, will take complete credit for every shot that lands roughly where it was intended—even if it bounced off a tree, winged a spectator, and was kicked into the hole by a wandering gypsy.

Golfers talk to balls (inanimate objects, let us remember), something no self-respecting savage would ever do. Many golfers, in fact, carry on extensive conversations which are not unlike liturgical chants, but yet are not much like them, either. Most address the ball at least twice—before and after swinging. Some players prefer carts to caddies because, unlike people, they do not count, criticize, or laugh.

Golf is not so much a game as it is a passionate faith that we will hit the ball a mile next time. It demands commitment and dedication. The person who takes up golf to get his mind off work often takes up work to get his mind off golf. Neither rain nor snow nor storm of night will turn him from his appointed rounds, although hurricanes and tornadoes have delayed some matches as long as an hour.

Golf builds character. For many it is a five-mile walk punctuated by disappointments. To improve one's game, intense discipline is required: one can take expensive lessons, practice constantly, or cheat. Where else (including church) can we meet three strangers, spend two intimate hours together, and return as enemies?

While choosing between golf and church on Sundays is a moral issue for some Christians, the game has brought a few backsliders home to the fold. These persons either want to commune with God, or they conclude that, playing no better than they do, they might as well go to church on Sundays.

Golf reveals our priorities. To paraphrase scripture, it does not always bring peace but a club—either a driver or a nine-iron. It reveals that a man's foes may be in his own household, as some wives (those who don't play themselves) regard emergency appendectomies and graduations from college as more important than golf matches.

To be fair, some people do not regard golf as a religion, and play only for the exercise. For them, breaking par is not the most important goal in life; it ranks no higher than third or fourth behind riches, fame, and two tickets to the Masters.

If golf is like religion, it is because it is also like life. The Christian religion has much to do with priorities, commitments, and relationships—not just rituals and "spiritual" matters. Golf, tennis, bridge, and churchgoing (!) can all become idolatrous *if* they become disproportionate in our lives.

There are golfing widows and churchgoing widowers. A tennis racket can divide a family and so can a committee. We are called to live our faith at work and play, at home and in church. Simple games can become significant events.

The intensity of our play reveals a lot about our values. A cartoon showed a red-faced golfer, livid with frustration and rage, screaming at his companion: "Stop saying it is just a game. It's not just a game!"

Thus, the choice for some of us is to decide which of our games are work—full of intensity and competition—and which are play—making little difference no matter whether we win or lose, or *how* we play them. And we must make sure our teammates and our opponents share a similar philosophy, for one person's game is another's war. Once priorities are clear, we can say, "Greater love hath no man than this: that he be willing to give up his golf game for family or faith as he walks down the fairways of life."

9
On Self-Denial
and Other Excesses

When Shakespeare warned us to "beware the ides of March," he could have had several dangers in mind. The month itself is totally unpredictable, and shedding heavy underwear too soon is an annual miscalculation many of us make. No one really objects to March coming in like a lion; it is its hanging around like a polar bear that's depressing.

Even so, the most difficult challenge to churchgoers in March is not the weather but Lent. Lent is an anachronism in an affluent society, a relic left over from the days of pre-television, pre-instant foods, and pre-Alka Seltzer. Or so we think.

That a season of self-discipline and self-denial is good for us is not the question. It is good for our health, if nothing else, particularly for those of us who regard heavy breathing after arriving at church as evidence of Christian commitment. No, our problem with Lent is the dilemma of practicing self-denial for a season while surrounded by the temptations of a consumer society. Self-denying activities, after all, are best reserved for saints-in-training hidden away in cloisters and far removed from every temptation that is really attractive.

The dilemma is keenest, for example, when persons vow to practice greater moderation in their eating habits. "No more desserts until Easter," he says determinedly on Ash Wednesday evening following pie a la mode. "Rye-crisp and lettuce for lunch for a month," she proclaims, deeply moved by a biography of St. Francis of Assisi. Goodies will be baddies for the duration of Lent, at the end of which time a penitent, well-disciplined, and skinnier Christian will emerge.

Such noble intentions are not made easy, however, by coffee breaks at which genial colleagues provide donuts in the same spirit Eve provided Adam his first apple. Nor do mothers-in-law help our drive for self-denial; their immortal words, "a tiny piece of pie can't hurt," are persuasive, especially if refusal means we'll be left out of her will. Furthermore, one should give up television if one is also giving up food; St. Francis was never exposed to commercials in living color promoting gluttony as an American virtue.

In short, those who would practice self-denial in our culture are beset on every side with invitations to indulge. We have not only to contend with the weaknesses of the flesh, which are considerable, but also with threats to family unity and loyalty to one's country. The situation is complicated by the fact that we probably made a *public* vow to be strong—usually in a moment of weakness.

Shopping in a modern supermarket becomes a test of willpower—a tug-of-war between a carefully created shopping list and hunger pangs most recently associated with survivors of the Bataan Death March. The dilemma is captured graphically by homemaker magazines which contain about the same number of recipes for sumptuous meals as they do new thirty-day diets.

The irony is that we call such exertions "fasting"— a practice that causes the season to drag at about the same pace as a child on the way to the dentist. "Slowing" would be a much better name. Indeed, the reason self-discipline is so hard to learn is that we need self-discipline in order to learn it. Self-denial, in other words, is a lot like going to sleep; trying harder to do it makes it harder to do.

One lesson, then, that temporary self-denial teaches is the realization that our lives are more self-indulgent than we thought. The old adage, "Hitting your head against a wall is a pleasure because it feels so good when you stop," has its Lenten counterpart: "Practicing self-discipline for a season is painful because it feels so bad when you start."

Nevertheless, we sometimes succeed and find ourselves practicing disciplined eating and exercise habits. Alas! We often discover that we have created a monster in the process. The only person who suffers more than a martyr or ascetic is the spouse of one. Will power, an admirable trait in ourselves, is frequently experienced as obstinancy by others. It may be that the primary virtue learned from fasting is long-suffering, especially by those who eat at the same table.

In other words Lent, like Christmas, must be practiced all year and not just for a season. Otherwise, we only learn when we've had enough after we've had too much. If, however, self-discipline and moderation are germane to our lifestyles and not mere appendages, they will neither hurt so much nor cry for attention so loudly.

A way of living that says "no" to indulgences also says "no" to the temptation to advertise one's lean and hungry look. Exceptions to one's life style, not the rules, beg for attention. The good news is that the ides of March will hold no terrors for us. We will be able to face the beginning of Lent without gritting our teeth and the end of it without hunger pangs.

10
Unhappy Are
the Hard-Boiled

J. B. Phillips says that much of the world believes the following: "Happy are the hard-boiled: for they never let life hurt them." *

Many Americans, in fact, have cultivated the hard-boiled image and made it a lifestyle. The media have done their share, too, even giving it a name: *machismo*. According to the Harper *Dictionary of Contemporary Usage, machismo* comes from the Spanish and means "masculinity." It is a vogue word for an "excessive display of action and attitudes which are supposed to demonstrate virility and masculinity." "Boldness, physical courage, aggressiveness, and domination over women" are marks of the "macho" man.

"Macho-men" walk tall and talk tough. They love 'em and leave 'em. Their shirts are worn open to the navel, and they wear razor blades on chains around their necks. For recreation they go hang-gliding or race fast cars on narrow roads. Give a "macho-man" a beer, and he'll swallow it in one gulp and crush the

---

Your God Is Too Small (Riverside, N.J.: Macmillan and Co., 1958), p. 101.

can one-handed. Treat him with the milk of human kindness, and he'll mix it with whiskey. Where does a 500 pound gorilla sleep at night? Next to a man with *machismo*—after he asks permission.

Middle-aged men appear a bit silly when they exhibit "macho" signs and symbols, even though many try. Shirts worn open to the fourth button may look sexy on Clint Eastwood, but when you have to color the hair on your chest with Grecian Formula 44, it's time to button up, Charlie. Nor do many of us over forty deliberately perform acts of physical courage, unless we can be finished with them and in bed by 10:30 P.M. Most of us of this age are more concerned with how *far* a car will go than how fast. Whatever aggressiveness is left is used keeping a child in college and ourselves out of debt.

More important than being conscious of the physical limitations of *machismo* is being aware that it is self-defeating. The ability to project it may diminish as, each year, we need more horsepower and less exhaust. But being hard-boiled is also inherently depressing.

There are many experiences of life which teach this lesson. Happy marriages demonstrate that mutual love beats sexual domination by a bushel and a peck and a hug around the neck. Sitting with a dying person takes a quiet strength that a leather jacket can never provide unless there's a Kleenex in the pocket. A father of four children has had his fling with virility, too.

For some of us, however, the lesson has been most vividly learned from being a father to daughters. This is not because little girls are delicate flowers, petite combinations of fluff and chromosomes too fragile for rough handling. Not at all. They're just as wiry, just as ornery, and just as resilient as their brothers.

No, the lesson is learned in the *relationship* between father and daughter—especially little daughters. Fathers often yield to the temptation to play macho-man with their sons. They squeeze the biceps of little boys to see how strong they're getting. Little boys are not supposed to cry; they are, after all, to be "little men." Fathers are less tempted to play this role with their daughters.

Our nine-year-old, in fact, taught her father that soft-boiled is better than hard-boiled any day. While riding double on her bike (against parental rules, of course), she and her friend landed in a heap with Ruthie on the bottom. The result was a badly bruised ego as well as severe cuts to the lower lip and point of the chin.

She came running home for help. Veteran parents, naturally, have seen so many cuts and bruises they know the staff of the hospital emergency room by their first names. So her mother stopped the flow of blood before it dripped on the rug and took her to the doctor for stitches. The remarkable fact, though, was that Ruthie did not shed a single tear during or after the accident.

The doctor who sewed her up commented, in fact, on her bravery. Ruthie's reply caught us by surprise: "My daddy told me once when I was hurt not to be a crybaby!"

Had I done that?!?! What kind of a hard-heart would inhibit his little girl from crying after a six-stitch accident? It's all right to cry when you're really hurt! What had I done?

My concern was completely transformed. Her cuts would heal, but would she go through life unable to cry because her father had taught her to be "tough?" At the first opportunity I went to console her but mainly to release her from the bondage my comment had caused.

"Ruthie," I began, groping for words. "I'm glad you were so brave at the doctor's office . . . uh, what I mean is . . . crying is O.K when you're hurt. Mom said you didn't cry when you should have . . . that is, you don't have to cry, but if you felt like it, nobody'd care."

Ruthie sat quietly, a puzzled look on her stitched-up face.

"Of course, *I'd* care, honey . . . no, not about your crying . . . I'd understand because we love you, and we know how much it hurts and. . . ."

A gleam of recognition glistened in her eye. Reaching out, she patted my hand. "It's all right, daddy. You can cry if you want to."

The hard-boiled are wrong. "Happy are they who bear their share of the world's pain: in the long run they will know more happiness than those who avoid it." *

---

* Phillips, *Your God Is Too Small,* p. 101.

11
Irresistible Forces
and Immovable Objects

The purpose of parenthood is to cut the cord, to push the birds out of the nest, to help a dependent person become independent. Seldom, however, does this occur suddenly and finally. Only in the book of Revelation is there a once-and-for-all cosmic battle that completes the task. Parenthood is a twenty-year struggle between irresistible forces and immovable objects.

What parents must understand is that the struggle is the *natural order of things*. They are not failing as parents or as Christians when their kids force encounters. The umbilical cord does not break neatly and cleanly. It stretches and shreds and wears thin until one day we discover our child has left the womb.

Parents whose children have left home and turned out all right sometimes forget the struggle that helped achieve "all-rightness." One mother, speaking of her grown daughter, commented, "My little Janie never gave me a minute's trouble when she was growing up." Such a statement requires interpretation. Janie probably gave her mother *hours* and *days* of trouble, not minutes, when she was a child. The fact that Janie reached adulthood without having been caught perpetrating any major crimes merely softened the memory.

The arenas for the struggle are several. Usually they're not very dramatic and involve skirmishes rather than atomic warfare. They center around such issues as the habitat (as in, "Please clean up your room") and dress (e.g. "That skirt is too short, dear."). The children's job is to push for *independence*, as their parents stand, arms akimbo, four-square for *responsibility*.

No family encounter illustrates the dynamics of the relationship more fully than when a daughter starts to date. Nothing makes the world beat a path to your door like a teenage daughter. And never is the relationship of parent and child so tested as when one of those path-beaters wants to take her out. While the teenage years are few in number, a dating daughter ages her parents by at least twenty years.

The beginnings of the process are often subtle, usually innocent, and frequently wholesome. Parents accustom themselves to groups of young people appearing early and staying late—doing homework, planning a meeting, or giggling. A feeding program, unbudgeted but comparable in scope to the Marshall Plan, becomes a daily occurrence. Parents are inclined to notice appetites at this point, and it is a matter of little consequence that some of the mouths are located in male bodies.

The day comes, however, when one member of the group hangs around long after the others have moved on to greater refrigerators of harvest. Parents may then notice that the hanger-on is a b-o-y, a fact that theretofore was of little significance until set in juxtoposition with the recollection that their daughter is a g-i-r-l. (Translation: "Is David *still* here *again* to-night?")

Eventually, the relationship is made public. It is announced that daughter and friend are "going together," which means they will spend all day attending the same classes in the same school and then hurry home to talk for hours on telephones to plan what they're going to do that night. Dating rapidly evolves from a short period when two people cannot see too much of each other into a long period when they do.

Conscientious parents, of course, feel called to intervene. Rules must be established and guidelines set down. A father, with studied casualness, initiates a thoughtful conversation with his daughter about Moral Responsibility—while his wife talks about all the good stuff. Signals are worked out so that messages can be delivered when suitors are lingering too long, e.g. "When I flush the toilet and gargle, it means he's got to leave!"

It is important that parents intervene, for without their interference many dating relationships would not move on to the next stage—The Struggle. After all, Romeo and Juliet had to contend with parents, and there is nothing wrong with teenagers today that parents' trying to reason with them won't aggravate.

The struggle may be internal to the couple itself, of course, since half the fun of being in love is the worry of it. Hours of conversation deal with whether one or the other has talked to, looked at, held hands with, or been seen in the presence of romantic competitors. Indeed, if people really did die from broken hearts, no teenaged girl would ever survive her first boyfriend.

Fortunately, young girls and young boys do recover from their romantic entanglements—what Robert

Frost called their "irresistible desire to be irresistibly desired." It is part of growing up, obviously, but to so describe it is not to demean the process. It is an important part, after all, and learning the difference between infatuation and love comes only with experience.

The task of the Christian parent is to provide a context for that experience, to be an authority against which teenagers can push, and to know when to scold and when to hold. At times it is a thankless task, but parents are sustained by the belief that their children will mature as a result of the process.

In sentimental moments fathers and mothers may even justify their interference with the hope that their daughters will be grateful to them one day. They may, in their maudlin moments, think their children will be so grateful as to take care of them when they're old— a condition which comes quickly when daughters start to date.

12
Joyful Noises
Slightly Off-Key

Family togetherness is not a prearranged grouping with an original and four carbon copies. It is more like the Body which Paul describes in the New Testament —an organic whole with members who perform various functions.

In our family there are four children—Sarah, Martha, Bret, and Ruth. We, as parents, attempt to influence them daily, but it's clear they are developing personalities beyond the scope of their parents' imaginations. They are gifts from God, not laboratory animals destined to respond to controlled environments and, thank God, not limited by family expectations.

Brand new parents discover this truth early. One of the author's colleagues, a fine athlete and lover of sports, eagerly awaited, with his wife, the birth of their first child. While he consistently proclaimed that he would cheerfully accept either a male *or* a female child, his friends were convinced nothing would make him happier than to have a boy—who would one day be an All-American basketball player.

As the chromosomes would have it, they had a girl.

We all wondered how Alan, in his heart of hearts, would respond? The answer came when he arrived to share his news. Wearing an enormous grin, he said, "You ought to see her hands. They're great! She'll be the best girl basketball player in Indiana!"

Furthermore, our children are "gifts" who possess "gifts." They have creative urges which, when expressed, demonstrate uniqueness but which sometimes melt the glue of family togetherness. Consider, for example, what happens when four children reveal a passion to play musical instruments.

Musical instruments surprise parents whose primary abilities in this area lie with the shoe horn. Music, of course, like apple pie and brotherhood, is a "good thing," and scripture certainly suggests it is a special gift.

> Sing praises to the Lord with the lyre,
>   with the lyre and the sound of melody!
> With trumpets and the sound of the horn
>   make a joyful noise before the King, the Lord!
>   (Ps. 98:5–6)

The Psalmist who wrote these words undoubtedly lived alone and never had a child in the next room practicing her violin. A careful reading of the text reveals no mention at all of the violin, an instrument which should never be played until a person knows how. Nor is there any specific reference to the clarinet, and few scholars presume that the phrase "sound of the horn" includes the clarinet—which is a strong argument for biblical literalism.

Our four children are currently playing or learning to play the piano, drum, clarinet, or violin. Even so, we hope they will grow up to love good music. The earliest stages, of course, are the most difficult for listeners, and a concert by beginners demonstrates little difference between music and the sounds associated with tuning instruments. Fortunately, only relatives ever attend such concerts, and they go to reassure themselves that their own offspring play badly for reasons other than faulty genes.

The violin can cause great agony in the early stages. When a child announces the desire to learn this instrument, parents may hear, in their mind's ear, the melodic sounds of the next Jascha Heifetz or Yehudi Menuhin. What they get, however, is a reminder that violin playing at its fundamental level is a process of pulling the hairs of a horse's tail across the intestines of a dead cat. At times, in fact, one gets the impression the cat is still alive!

Clarinets produce vibrant sounds that excite our emotions, and a Benny Goodman is able to mystify huge audiences with his skill. Many children learning to play clarinets mystify their parents, who wonder how such an expensive instrument could produce a sound not unlike the scraping of a fingernail across a chalkboard.

A drum, in the confines of a medium-sized home, sounds the same both early and late in a musician's career—*very loud. The* first thing that a child learns after he gets a drum is that he's never going to get another.

Studies of the effect of drum-playing on property values have not been made, nor have any scientific connections between it and the abandonment of children been established. If, however, *internal* feelings of neighbors and parents are considered, the biblical connection between anger and murder becomes apparent.

Piano-playing is a different tune. The quality of the noise it produces is usually tolerable even when it's

bad. The problem is that a child learns piano by playing a particular piece of music over and over and over.
And over again. Children have been known to resist
the discipline inherent in practicing the piano, and
many of them dislike the process immensely because
—if you'll pardon the pun—it's all work and no play.

Why, then, with the exception of a few homes
wherein prodigies bloomed or parents were deaf, do
adults persist in paying the price of music-making?
Not for financial gain, for what does it profit a parent
if he gains the whole world and loses his hearing? Nor
for fame, as first clarinet in a school orchestra will
generally earn less recognition than second-string
halfback on a losing football team.

Most do it because to encourage children to nurture
a gift—musical or otherwise—is worth the price.
Music we play, even poorly, enables us to express a
creative urge within ourselves. To fail to express that
gift—great or small—is to die a little prematurely.

Such a fate is a sad one and far more poignant than
the pain of a violin and a clarinet playing together
off-key. And that, music lovers, is *very* sad, indeed.

13
Up Close,
I'm Something Special

Despite considerable evidence to the contrary, Americans cling to a belief in inevitable progress. Some progress has been achieved, obviously, but it is by no means inevitable and some of its side effects are worse than backwardness.

Technology is supposed to be our servant, but we take orders from it. We are told not to fold, spindle, or mutilate, and we obey. The machines we created to save time are so expensive we work extra hours and second jobs to pay for them. They break down a lot, too, and even when they work they're not very friendly.

A telephone call was once a personal experience. We heard a human voice with a southern drawl or a New England twang. During those inefficient moments when a long distance call was going through, a small joke or a friendly remark might be shared. In small towns, in fact, the switchboard operators were known and all-knowing.

Now we have to memorize an access code, an area code, and seven digits. When dialed correctly, as happens on occasion, the phone treats us to a variety of hums, buzzes, and crackles—followed by a recording that tells us we have twenty seconds to leave a message at the sound of a beep. Numbers dialed incorrectly produce a jeering whine, a condescending voice telling us to redial, and the inner temptation to curse an inanimate object.

Jet airplanes have reduced travel time and increased waiting time. Terminals are places for interminable delays, filled with rows of plastic chairs so arranged as to prohibit efforts at conversation by any humans who are not also contortionists. Superhighways have alleviated the old frustration of traveling slowly through town after town on curving two-lane roads. Now we can drive for miles and never see a town except as we look down on houses from elevated inner loops. We accept the fact that we will have to drive fifteen miles if we want to turn around.

Computers symbolize the regressive nature of progress. Students in big universities have received mail which begins: "Dear 443–82–0356: We have a personal interest in you." Our zip-coded mail brings us information we don't want and advertisements for products we don't need—addressed to "occupant." Other mail with our very own names and addresses comes from lists that one agency sells to another. Indeed, there is little comfort in knowing that at this very moment someone, somewhere, is putting your name or mine on another mailing list.

The problem is common to us all: how do we live personally, humanely, and familiarly in a computerized world?

Some say we should resist progress for the sake of our own individuality. Deliberately fold, spindle, and mutilate your IBM card! Refuse to dial directly! Al-

ways call Information and talk with a human being!
Avoid exact change lanes!

More important, however, will be our willingness
to pay the price—the cost in extra time, inconvenience
and money. Technology cannot take away our humanity any more than plastic bars do a prison make.

We preserve humaneness by being humane in our
dealing with others. We can carry on a friendly conversation with a clerk as she checks the authorization
number on our credit card. We can be individuals because we are, after all, children of God who is like a
Father, not a great Computer in the sky.

The power to be free comes from the knowledge of
our acceptance by God as individuals. Dr. Seuss, that
great teacher-entertainer of children (and of those
parents who keep their children awake so as to read
his books longer), says it best:

If you'd never been born, well then what would you be?
You might be a fish! Or a toad in a tree!
You might be a doorknob! Or three baked potatoes!
You might be a bag full of hard green tomatoes!
Or worse than all that . . . why, you might be a
WASN'T!
A Wasn't has no fun at all. No, he doesn't.
A Wasn't just isn't. He just isn't present.
But you . . . you ARE YOU! And now, isn't that pleas-
ant!

.   .   .   .

Today you are you! That is truer than true!
There is no one alive who is you-er than you!
Shout loud, "I am lucky to be what I am!
Thank goodness I'm not just a clam or a ham!
Or a dusty old jar of sour gooseberry jam!

I am what I am! That's a great thing to be!
If I say so myself, "HAPPY BIRTHDAY TO ME!" *

Up close, impersonal world, I'm something special
—and so are we all.

---

* From *Happy Birthday to You!* by Dr. Seuss. Copyright ©
1959 by Dr. Seuss. Reprinted by permission of Random House,
Inc.

14
Too Much Civilization

Mark Twain once wrote, "Civilization is a limitless multiplication of unnecessary necessities." His words remind us not to mistake comfort for civilization, for when that happens the highest form of civilization is the people who can endure it.

Some people, in fact, have decided that the best way to endure it is to escape it. It is as if civilization might have been all right up to a point, but it went on too long. Thus, we continually experiment with ways to make the things we eat, drink, and wear as good as they used to be.

We may not be consciously aware that we resent encroaching civilization, but our actions speak louder than our conscious minds. We go camping to get away from it all, discovering in the process so many others with the same desire we get in the way of each other getting away from it all. Or we take long walks in the woods, if we can find a woods that doesn't require a half-hour drive to get there—and isn't posted "No Trespassing." When all else fails, as it often does, we turn to middle-class America's most frequent witness against civilization—the backyard cookout.

In ancient times meat burned outdoors was an act of
sacrifice. Nowadays it means somebody in the neigh-
borhood is having a cookout. Thirty years ago, only
hobos went in for outdoor cooking, but the invention of
the patio changed all that. It has provided a place
where we can burn leaves in the fall and hamburgers
in the summer.

To cook out in the backyard, modern man and modern woman deliberately reject modern kitchens with
their automatic lights and "pingers" guaranteeing
perfectly done food with the least possible trouble. It is
as if we shake our fists in the face of technology, determined to show that the spirit of adventure—or
masochism—is not dead.

Starting a charcoal fire, for example, has become an
art form. The ancient adage, "Where there's smoke,
there's fire," was coined before charcoal was packaged
and sold in grocery stores. Backyard chefs wonder
what it is about a fire that makes it so eager to start
in a forest and so reluctant to catch hold in a specially
designed grill holding carefully arranged briquets
that have been drenched in combustible fluid sufficient
to burn the cities of New York and Chicago.

The end result of fire-starting labors is either failure or success, each of which produces its own dilem-
mas. The sight of a grown man kneeling by a pile of
smoking coals and blowing with all his might at one
flickering spark provides both comic relief and sure
evidence that dinner will be late.

Success brings mixed results, too. A brightly glow-
ing charcoal fire inevitably produces clouds of smoke
sufficient to guide the Israelites by day and a fire so
hot that choices in meat are quickly reduced to two:
"well done" or "destroyed."

The smoke, of course, keeps mosquitos away, a

blessing not to be regarded lightly, as they often are the best-fed attenders of a cookout. Furthermore, those closest to the fire are seldom permanently blinded by the smoke, and it is well known that crying cleans out the tear ducts.

Eventually, the food is declared ready to eat—whether it is or not. People whose appetites have been titillated for over an hour by the smell of hamburger which has dropped through the grill onto the coals adjust their standards for food preparation considerably. Light-headedness due to empty-stomachedness and an ant crawling up one's leg also encourage a readiness to eat.

Backyard cookouts provide clear evidence that the human spirit craves some values civilization cannot provide. We want nutrition, but not too much. We want sanitary conditions, but not all the time. We desire comfort and convenience, but not at the expense of fellowship and shared adventure.

Cooking out brings family and friends together in a way that eating in often fails to do. Little children can smear and spill and be spared the wrath of their parents. The dog is a welcome attender and usually gets leftovers far more pleasing to his canine culinary criteria than packaged stuff that makes its own gravy.

For a few moments, at least, we confront our cellophane-wrapped culture and say, "We'd rather do it ourselves." Like the ancient Israelites, we follow fire and cloud to a promised land of Togetherness and Fellowship. That is a pilgrimage well worth taking, especially if we can find some manna to sustain us until the charcoal gets hot.

15
Hurrah
for Amateurs!

The quality of music and drama we hear and see today is probably no better than it was before television innundated our lives. It may be worse. However, the packaging of the performances is clearly better and, as a result, we have come to expect smoother and glossier productions.

Hidden microphones project the actor's voice, whether or not what is being said is worth hearing. Elaborate sets create the illusion of being where the theater program says the drama is taking place, and the price of the tickets is so high we could have chartered a plane and gone there. Off-camera, electronic cue cards protect performers from forgetting their lines, even if they are eminently forgettable.

The highest compliment we muster for an off-Broadway play or a way, way off-Broadway performance—such as in Richmond, Indiana—is to say it was "near professional." And the unkindest cut of all is to label your local civic theater performance "amateurish."

Except. Except on the day your child delivers a

crumpled, mimeographed note from the teacher announcing the annual, all-school Christmas program. Parents soon learn that the date and time for this event are more sacred than High Mass at St. Peter's, and woe unto a father or mother who fails to attend for any reason. Even death by hanging will be taken as a personal affront.

Temptations *not* to attend, however, are legion. Foremost is the rehearsal experience at home, better known as "learning your part." When, after hours of coaching, a child finally learns four lines of verse, parents rejoice. However, they then discover that a recitation of those four lines fifteen times a day for six weeks is more than enough opportunity for grasping their deepest meaning.

Other children, usually in the sixth grade, are "cool" about their performance. Two nights before the program a twelve-year-old may announce, "Say, Mom, I've got the lead in the Christmas play at school on Friday." Mother, a woman who in other circumstances is a witty and charming conversationalist, will barely manage a garbled (though loud, and with feeling) response: "You've got the *what* in the *which*, *where* on *when?*"

The dialogue from that point makes the Spanish Inquisition seem innocent. Suddenly, the family honor for four generations is in jeopardy if that boy doesn't know his lines. All other family activities come to a screeching halt. Older siblings become tutors. Father is sent to J. C. Penney's to buy yards of red and green material so that Mother can sew a costume, Edith Head not being available due to movie commitments. If a star is to be born, it will be by Caesarean section and require lots of stitches.

The Christmas program comes, ready or not. Each

class marches smartly to place, directed by teachers who have mastered the art of smiling broadly while warning Tony out of the corner of their mouths to stop stepping on the swaddling clothes the Virgin Mary is dragging behind her on the way to the manger. Wise men, dressed in their fathers' bathrobes, compete for platform space with shepherds wearing gunny-sack tunics over swim trunks and homemade sandals with shoestring laces.

The quality of the performance equals that of the costumes and demonstrates the mysterious truth that the whole is greater than the sum of its parts. Six children in the front row of the second grade chorus with one tooth missing present a scene more than six times as fascinating as one child without a tooth. An entire group of children singing off-key removes any anxiety a parent has about a child's distinctive monotone.

Mostly what Christmas programs have that professional performances can never match is audience rapport. No person ever attends such programs who is not related to at least one performer. In fact, the quality of such shows is irrelevant, although some are less painful than others. Parents witness the miracle of seeing their own children neatly dressed and temporarily clean. Half the fun is pointing out to grandparents Bret's location in the chorus: "See, there he is in the second row, the fourth reindeer from the end, right next to the girl in the red dress picking her nose." The other half the fun is in discovering your child's eyes, that moment when she sees you and you see her, and both know all is well.

Even though—in the name of separation of church and state—we have snowflakes instead of shepherds and "Jingle Bell Rock" in place of "Silent Night," such programs may still be sacred occasions. There is the holy experience of *caring* in the midst of a crowd. There is the cleansing feeling that comes as we accept the offerings children bring without judgment. And there is, once again, that mystical awareness that we are saved by the Grace of God and not by the quality of our performances. This, especially, is good news to all, particularly for those who can't carry a tune or remember their lines.

16
Keeping Up
with Upkeep

Robert Frost wrote: "Home is the place where, if you have to go there, they have to take you in." Home-*owners*, however, define "home" differently. For them, it is the place where, if you live there, something has to be fixed.

Part of the American Dream has long included vine-covered cottages and split-level suburbans. Darn! Upon awakening, the dreamer discovers how difficult it is to paint windows overgrown with vines and how expensive to fix split roofs of the split levels. Houses built to provide a little security for a family provide a lot of security for the banks which make home improvement loans.

Some homeowners who are, as the saying goes, "handy around the house," attempt major repairs and improvements themselves. A few among this number are talented craftsmen and inspire others of us to remodel or repair our own house. This pleases professional carpenters, plumbers, and electricians because they know it generates business for themselves.

The problem is that many homeowners who do-it-themselves reverse the intended order of things. Instead of first learning how and then doing it, many do-it-yourselfers first do and then learn how. Give an average homeowner the proper tools, and in a few minutes a leak in the toilet will turn into a flowing stream. Given more time and power equipment, a typical inexperienced homeowner can transform a simple task into a major disaster.

Therefore, for fixing things around the house, nothing beats a person who is handy with a checkbook. It takes a heap o' livin' to make a house a home, and it takes a heap o' spendin' to keep it repaired. We're never more conscious that our homes are our castles than when we pay a plumber, two carpenters, and an electrician to remodel a bathroom.

Whereas do-it-yourselfers *create* problems, professionals *discover* them. Putting in a shower will inevitably require moving the toilet eight inches. Moving the toilet means tearing up the floor. Fixing the floor takes a long time because the carpenter is on another job. Which means our friendly homeowner has a torn-up bathroom in his friendly home three weeks longer than he had planned. Which is a long time to go without a shower. Which makes it harder to stay friendly.

Major home improvements, such as insulation and new siding, sometimes get finished, and a new dilemma rears its redecorated head. What happens when, instead of tinkering to keep up with the Joneses, you become Jones? How does your life change when, suddenly and dramatically, your old house looks new?

Cars that slowed down as they passed your house were not unknown BNS (Before New Siding), but now their occupants nod approvingly instead of snorting and muttering "disgraceful." One becomes used to strangers appearing suddenly to feel the vinyl siding or rub, lovingly, the white trim. Living in a reborn house is much like being a Grand Champion heifer at the county fair.

Temptations to vanity are very real. Basking in the shadow of an attractive house—especially after never having had one before—is heady stuff. The magic words "how nice your house looks" transforms upkeep into keeping up.

Thankfully, your children and your friends neutralize tendencies toward egomania. The kids still use the side of the house to bounce the basketball off before driving in for a lay-up. Friends are relieved to discover, as one put it, that "the inside looks the same as ever" (Translation: "cluttered, needing paint, and with a crack in the dining room wall").

Scripture, if interpreted broadly enough, also speaks to this condition. It reminds us to keep our housing priorities in order. The rich man who tore down his old barns and built new ones is a case in point. Jesus reminded us that foxes have holes and birds have nests but he had nowhere to lay his head. Hence, he had no upkeep to ruin his weekends.

Good stewardship of possessions requires that we keep our property repaired, but seeking God's Kingdom still comes first. The message remains clear: Christ's presence in our home is more important then how keen it looks or how well it functions. His house is to be a house of prayer.

Besides, what will it profit us if we have wall-to-wall carpeting, wall-to-wall windows, and back-to-the wall financing?

17
We Are
Where We Eat

Eating is one of the acceptable indulgences for Christians. Many of us were brought up to believe that certain activities were not options for us. We weren't allowed to drink, dance, or hit night spots. A childhood jingle stated the matter succinctly: "We don't smoke, and we don't chew, and we don't go with girls who do."

Eating, however, is a sanitary pleasure, made acceptable by the lifestyle of Jesus who was a charming guest at the Cana wedding feast and who enjoyed goodies provided by Martha, Peter's mother-in-law, and Zaccheus. We may recall, particularly after a sumptuous meal, that Jesus was unfairly criticized for mingling with an *eating* as well as a drinking crowd. Sermons on temperance were always directed toward those who drank booze, and seconds or thirds on dessert were virtuous efforts to make a hostess feel good.

Shoot! There are always those about who remind us that eating has moral dimensions just like "real" vices. There are mothers who counsel their children to clean their plates because villagers in South America are starving. Eating everything on a plate does little to help villagers, however, and many children would happily send their broccoli to them by direct mail.

Other reminders come from vegetarians who speak softly without a big steak. Occasionally, we will be asked to fast for the good of our souls, at which time it is helpful to be able to quote 1 Timothy 6:17, which speaks of "the living God, who giveth us richly all things to enjoy" (KJV).

That verse will probably not succeed in squelching the vegetarians and the fasters, and it also fails to speak to the way in which eating has come to have important *symbolic* meaning in American society. Unwritten but real class distinctions are structured around what we eat, where we eat it, and what we're supposed to be wearing while eating.

To be "sophisticated" is to appreciate gourmet cooking. It is to tell friends of our most recent discovery of little (never big) restaurants which are either "quaint" (with scenes of Paris on the wall) or "adorable" (frilly curtains on the windows). Such places don't serve food but "cuisine," and it is hinted that if you cannot pronounce the name of the dishes on the menu, you probably cannot afford to eat there. Indeed, if prices are not listed on the menu at all, you can know in your heart of hearts (and your pocketbook of pocketbooks) that you have either *arrived* or misread the directions to McDonalds.

It should not surprise us that there are industries which rate and rank restaurants around the world. Well-paid persons travel from city to city, sampling *hors d'oeuvres* and testing the menu. Restaurant owners compete for the best chefs the way baseball teams compete for free agents. The degree of exclusiveness in the dining experience is often determined numerically: How many stories high is the restaurant located? How many waiters per table? How many forks are provided per course?

At its best, dining in a superb restaurant enables us to eat carefully prepared food in a pleasant atmosphere. For some parents, eating where there are cloth napkins and glass glasses is a well-deserved reward for all the hamburgers and milkshakes they've endured the rest of the time. At its worst, however, eating out in order to impress feeds the temptation to look down on others. It is to pay expensive prices because it is fashionable, or vice versa.

Retribution has a way of coming, even when our indulgences are on the middle-class approved list. When we eat rich food, we gain weight or acquire pimples or get gastritis. If we attempt to gain status by our eating habits, we discover that exclusive dinner parties are frequently amateur expressions of self-inflicted boredom. A tasteful little buffet turns out to be merely a dinner where the guests outnumber the chairs, and many crimes have been committed in the name of "cuisine."

Let's face it, fellow diners. No indulgence is safe from its own special temptations. Jesus ate here and there with one group or another, demonstrating in the meanwhile that life is more important than food—or where we eat it, or with which fork in which restaurant with how many stars after its name. We do well to remember, at least three times a day, that food is made for people and not people for food. Hungering for the Bread of Life will keep our eating priorities in order.

18
Heroes
and Heroines

Our facination with America's "Beautiful People" has no observable limits. We wear Farrah Fawcett Majors T-shirts and are titillated by what she wears —or doesn't wear—to bed. If Robert Redford sneezes, a thousand noses sniffle in sympathy. Our children eat Crunchy-Wunchies because O. J. Simpson has them for breakfast, and one writer did an in-depth study of Muhammad Ali's garbage—to find out what he was "really like." We are, evidently, what we throw away.

The media hath made the beautiful people beautiful, of course, and the media can taketh them away. Out of sight they quickly become out of mind, and new creations appear. Thus, even though our appetites for news of their comings and goings are insatiable, we err when we take them seriously, especially when we use them for models.

My fellow Americans, we need—not more Beautiful People—but authentic, untarnished heroes. The persons for whom the media provide the greatest visibility are seldom paragons of virtue, and few among the multitudes who follow the adventures of Cher and

Liz with fascination (or even adulation) really want their children to become one.

Nor are the never-ending exposes of police and political corruption edifying experiences for young or old. Rumor has it, in fact, that in one large city wherein the police department is infamous for its corruption, children have been playing cops and cops instead of cops and robbers!

If athletes once played the game for honor, glory, or a crippled child in the hospital, now they do or die for stock options and fringe benefits. An entire issue of *Sport Magazine* was recently devoted to the sex lives of unmarried athletes, and several of its articles glorified the bedroom exploits of professional football and baseball players. "Scoring" has taken on a new meaning.

Would you believe: The winner of a recent all-American soap box derby was discovered to have cheated, thereby receiving some criticism but also several expressions of grudging approval for the cleverness of his idea. Not even soap-related events, it seems, are 99.44 percent pure!

Thus, we may breathe a sigh of relief when the calendar reminds us of "real" heroes from times past. February brings the comforting memories of Washington and Lincoln, around whom time, distance, and tradition have built a wall of honor and respect. The story of "Honest Abe" walking miles through the snow to return a few pennies due an overcharged customer warms our hearts, especially when clerks today would just as soon we didn't bother, since it messes up the credit billing.

We love, also, to recount for young children how George Washington couldn't tell a lie when he confessed to his father that, indeed, he had cut down the cherry tree. Of course, *his* father probably hadn't been nurturing it like a baby for five years, either, the way today's backyard farmers do.

The point is, faithful readers, that most heroes and heroines "up close" lose some of their luster. Our selective memories enable us to overlook the fact that Washington owned slaves and Lincoln was a practitioner of politics at a very earthy level. Given the mood of our times, in fact, we should not be surprised to learn someday that Horatio Alger cheated on his income tax!

Most sobering of all, however, is the realization that for our children, our friends, and our acquaintances, we are so close at hand that the chance to be a *great* example—to be a hero or heroine to somebody—ranges between slim and zero. A *very* small child will revere father and mother until she learns better, and a neighbor may regard us with respect and admiration until our dog gets into his garbage can.

Nor will we get many dramatic opportunities to demonstrate courage and integrity. Few of us will get the chance to face Bad Guys in Black Hats at High Noon. Instead, we will have to deal daily with small skirmishes—the temptation to tell modest lies to the boss, to take out our anger on our children, or to goof off on the job. The probability is that we will have our courage tested more by delivering our son's newspapers in the rain than in crossing the Delaware to save a revolution.

Even so, this is the real stuff of exemplary living. We can't depend on anyone else, even George and Abe, to provide models. As anonymous as our lives are compared to Dick and Liz, Gerald and Betty, Jimmy and Rosalyn (note the political impartiality), Joe, O. J., or Sonny and Cher, they are far more visible—and far more instructive—to people close to us. If we choose to be Christian, we have no alternative. We are called to live as obediently as we can, even though the celebration of our birthdays will never give Americans a day off from work.

19

In Praise of
"Old" Lovers

Ever since a poet first rhymed *June* with *moon*, the sixth month has been glorified as a time for romantic fulfillment, complete with wedding bells and trousseaus. Most who get married are, of course, much too young, as a glance at one's own wedding pictures twenty years later clearly reveals. Indeed, a case could be made for the belief that love is the last and most serious childhood disease.

Nevertheless, this chapter is a tribute to love, but not—let us hasten to add—"young love." September is supposed to be the month for middle-aged lovers, the inference being that falling leaves symbolize fading passions. We feel otherwise, holding that love and education are alike in that it is a shame to waste them on the young.

It is easy to understand love at first sight, but how do we explain it after two people have been looking at each other for twenty years or more? The person who has been married for *many years* knows far more about love than the person who has been married *many times*. Love, after all, is like a mushroom: we can never tell if it is the real thing until it is too late.

If romance is like a long, sweet dream, marriage is the alarm clock. It awakens us to real life and real love. In fact, the course of true love never runs smooth —if it leads to marriage. Marriage—as its veterans know well—is the continuous process of getting used to things you hadn't expected. This fact helps explain why there are so many divorces. Slight acquaintances sharing romantic notions often get married, but a couple really has to know each other to get divorced!

Still, the main point is that middle-aged love between wives and husbands can be, and often is, every bit as romantic (and as much fun) as that of any young couple still finding rice in their pockets. If the "cure" for love is marriage, the "cure" for marriage is love again—and again and again. George Gene Nathan once commented that a man may be said to love most truly that woman in whose company he can feel drowsy in comfort. Resting in the security that comes from not having to impress each other, couples married twenty years are free to enjoy each other's idiosyncrasies.

Contrary to youthful opinion, a happily married couple still makes love. One survey discovered that teenagers assumed their parents seldom had sexual relations and that people over forty had almost no sex life.

Good. Let them think what they want. It inspires the young to think they discovered romance all by themselves, and it may provide some luxurious privacy if children assume their parents go to bed just to get extra rest.

If our children are fortunate and have happy marriages, the natural order of things will prevail and they'll learn the truth about love. They'll discover, when the time comes, that love is more than an itchy feeling around the heart that can't be scratched. Old lovers do not have to be sexual gymnasts with one another; familiarity breeds contentment. Unlike old dogs, they can learn new tricks but they will enjoy the old ones they've been playing for twenty years.

Romance is best in long marriages because it does not depend upon its own fires of passion to be sustained. It is nurtured by respect, for in a happy marriage there are two people unworried about who's the better half. A happy marriage is the union of two good forgivers, and many a couple does more than kiss (eh! eh!) and make up after a disagreement.

Good marriages are not made in heaven. They come in kits and we have to put them together ourselves. In order to have a good spouse, you have to be one. Romantic love in a mature marriage occurs in spite of faults, not just because of virtues. Happy marriages begin when we marry the ones we love, and they blossom when we love the ones we marry.

Cheers for young love! There's nothing quite like it. Thank God it doesn't last, however. Thank God it becomes "old love" which is just right for folks over forty. They know they have something special—each other—without whom they could not have stood married life. And they know old lovers never die; they just kiss away—at least until their kids return home and catch them necking in the dark.

20
The Lord Loves
a Cheerful Crusader

The question is: Can we save the world and laugh about it at the same time? Are we able to demonstrate a serious purpose and a lighthearted attitude?

Many cannot. Thoreau said, "If a man has a pain in his bowels, he forthwith sets about reforming the world." It seems that the motive behind some world-savers is their joy in suppressing joy, and many reformers would like to turn the world into a reformatory.

A grim disposition—let us hasten to add—may be an acceptable price to pay for important social reforms. Those of us who make the best of things seldom try to make them better. And the people who benefit from reforms—the hungry who are fed, the children freed from sweatshops, the black people who can eat at lunch counters—care little about how cheerful the crusaders who help set them free are.

Even so, the point is that a grim disposition is not necessarily the traveling companion of reform. Carrie Nation may have been the life of the party when she wasn't hacking up saloons. Abraham Lincoln is re-

membered for his social passion and his quick wit.
John Bunyan felt that seriousness and gaiety had been
joined by God and ought not to be put asunder by man.
Jeremiah . . . well, Jeremiah was probably a pain in
the neck all the time.

For most of us, however, our problem is a deficiency
on both sides of the issue. We have too little social
passion and too much grumpiness when we dabble in
causes. For example, the so-called cheerful giver to
worthy causes is an endangered species. To be fair,
any persons who have given out of generosity to one
cause may have their spirits dampened by the deluge
of requests from other crusades. This writer alone has
received over three hundred requests in a year for
donations, which is like asking a family on welfare to
take in an orphan.

Our mail indicates that there is a reform movement
for every problem and a support group for each need.
Letters come from Save the Whale Fund, Save The
Redwoods League, the Oceanic Society (save the
oceans), American Littoral Society (save the coast-
lines), Environmental Action (save the environment),
the Cousteau Society (save marine life), Defenders of
Wildlife (save the wildlife), and the Wilderness Society (save the wilderness for the wildlife).

Some of the requests conflict with each other. It
makes little sense to support Gun Owners of America
(save the guns) and the Committee for Hand Gun
Control. Someone who wants to contribute to all requests, furthermore, will face a real dilemma when an
appeal from the AFL-CIO arrives the same day as
one from AAUCG (Americans Against Union Control
of Government).

Other requests come from organizations with names
that are difficult to oppose. We are inclined to favor a

Fund for World Rehabilitation, for the more we see of this world, the less we fear the next. Even so, how much will a two-dollar contribution help rehabilitate the world? Or our nation? Or town? Actually, we could spruce up the front yard a bit for two bucks.

Few of us are unsympathetic to the cause represented by Americans Opposed to High Taxes or Bibles for the World. Granted, we need more information from the Population Institute before we give, as we need to know whether it is *for* more children, *against* more children, or suggesting ways to get rid of the ones we have.

The cheerful giver and the cheerful crusader share a common dilemma. Where can we put our dollars and our passions cheerfully and enthusiastically?

That question, of course, is extraordinarily personal, but there are some clues to guide us. Do we *hurt* when we see or hear of a concern or crusade? Oddly enough, we'll cheerfully give money or energy to those causes in which we feel personally involved. If we can imaginatively identify with hungry people, poor people, whales, or the wilderness, we'll ask, "How much can I give?" not, "Do I have to?"

Does it seem a *right* thing to support? This is a different question from "will it do any good?" A Christian perspective frees us to act because our actions demonstrate obedience to God's will, not because we can expect tangible results. If spraying with hydrocarbons breaks down the ozone layer in God's creation, then we ought to use a pump spray, even though the ozone layer will not be affected much by one individual's action. It may, of course, *lead* to a reform, for as Emerson said, "Every reform was once a private opinion." The point is that *cheerful* reforming comes from doing the right thing for the right reasons.

Are we aware of our shortcomings in *other* areas? The fact is, we don't always do the right thing, nor are we always appreciative of others when they practice "rightness" about which we aren't concerned. It's hard to save the whales when we're committed to saving the jobs of the whalers. The moralist, as over against the cheerful crusader, always knows better than others what's bad for them. The moralist never runs out of ideas as to how other people ought to change.

We will be able to walk cheerfully over the land, carrying on the crusades to which we are called, when we are able to see people as they are—a little lower than the angels but at times only a bit higher than the apes. Cheerful crusaders are cheerful lovers of humanity—warts and all—and they relate to the human race as if they belonged to it.

21
Living
Can Be Hazardous
to Your Health

Each new day brings reports of dangers to life on our planet. Just about everything we put into our mouths has been linked to a disease or an ailment. Too many eggs means too much cholesterol. Sugar stimulates hyperactivity in children, news which is as welcome to parents as water to a drowning man. Sugar substitutes have been linked with cancer in rats, and coffee may affect blood pressure.

Vitamin C was and may still be good for us, but scientists have discovered dangerous side effects. Oranges, therefore, are now suspect and may be stamped with the warning, "A Day Without Orange Juice May Be Good For You." Gloomy headlines regularly spoil our appetites, e.g. *California Researchers Link Peanut Butter To Bronchial Asthma*. One man became so depressed from reading about connections between eating habits and health he gave up reading.

Junk foods have been identified not only as poor in nutrients but as a factor in difficulties ranging from psoriasis to impotence to lycanthropy (werewolfism!) Our minds are at ease if the only danger our food purchases represent is "possible brain damage"—the first sign of which is a mind at ease. Indeed, if we kept every food hazard out of the reach of children, our refrigerators would be empty and our cupboards bare.

Eating is merely the most obvious threat to health. Aerosols are destroying the atmosphere's ozone layer, letting in deadly ultraviolet rays. Rock music, played long enough and loudly enough, damages our hearing —which might not be so bad considering what's currently being played. We are literally swimming in pollution—chemical, sonic, or electromagnetic. The best way to keep healthy is to eat what we don't want, drink what we don't like, and do what we'd rather not.

Or so it seems. The problem with taking all the advice and all the fears seriously is that it makes hypochondriacs of us all. Indeed, with so many dangers to health being advertised in the news media, a new category of mental illness has been identified: paranoid hypochondria. This neurosis describes persons who fear things are not as bad as they've been reported.

Many of us share paranoid hypochondria. Americans worry about their health too much. Research which tentatively discovers a new link between heart disease and something we like makes its way into the popular press partly because we enjoy reading about gloom. Just as we share a compulsion to look at pictures of earthquakes and flock to disaster movies, we are fascinated by the latest threat to our liver or bowels. True, we may resent listening to hypochondriacs reciting their ailments, but the reason may be that they are telling their pains before we can tell ours.

This writer, a diabetic, is familiar with the temptation to share the up-to-date news of his disease with all who care to listen—a much smaller number than he had hoped. Indeed, if one rejoices in discussing one's illness, diabetes is an exceptional disease to have. It is serious enough to win enormous amounts of attention, (scarcely a week goes by without a story about diabetes in the popular press) but able to be controlled with reasonable care.

The best time to be a diabetic is at the dinner table when you refuse dessert. This invariably prompts the question, "Are you on a diet?" The standard reply is, "No, my pancreas doesn't work," and from there the diabetic can dominate the table conversation for the next twenty minutes. It is a fact that the author has gotten more conversational mileage out of his pancreas after it stopped working than he ever did while it was functioning.

By interjecting the word *pancreas* we open a whole new dimension. Diabetics can then discuss knowledgeably the whole range of their illness, from the causes of the disease through how the pancreas works to the hazards of insulin shock. At our worst we may carry a slide showing a cross-section of the pancreas to be used as a visual aid during conversation. There is no guarantee, however, that you will have much use for it on subsequent occasions, mostly because others will avoid conversations the way diabetics avoid sweets.

Nor is it a particularly effective way to enjoy life. Real hypochondriacs can't leave being well, well enough alone. They go through life on their death beds. When they—and we—worry too much about health, less time is left to enjoy it. Hypochondria is itself an illness in which the more you think, the more you think you need a doctor.

We do well to remember that good health, at best, lasts only a lifetime. The British historian, Kenneth

Clark, puts it this way: "Our days are numbered even in the best of times." There is a line which divides reasonable care of ourselves from nervous preoccupation with the care and feeding of our bodies. There is a difference between treating our bodies as "temples of God" and worrying constantly about repairs on the temple.

Jesus told the hypochondriac to take up his bed and walk. He also encouraged temperate, moderate living. The two commands do not contradict each other. They merely indicate that there is more enjoyment to be gained from good health than from preoccupation with ailments. The best medicine for rheumatism is to give thanks it isn't gout, and the best way to avoid the hazards of living is to give thanks for life, even if your pancreas doesn't work.

22
Why the Reaper
Is Grim

Ruth Ackerman Mullen, my brother's wife, lost a long and courageous bout with cancer at age forty-two. As executive director of the Queensboro Society for the Prevention of Cruelty to Children in New York City, her life had been one of service. Every working day was to deal with a traumatized child whose body or mind, or both, had been tortured by disturbed adults.

She did her work nobly and intelligently, transcending bureaucratic red tape to demonstrate practical love and compassion for brutalized children. Nevertheless, she—like all others—was not immunized from death by her goodness, and on October 15, 1969, she died in a New York hospital with her husband, Frank, by her side.

During her final days Ruth had tended to both serious and trivial concerns. She made regular telephone calls to the office, checking on details but primarily making sure that her "temporary" replacement could carry on effectively. And she kept one ear glued to the radio, listening intently and often giving a weak cheer for her beloved New York Mets as they battled for the World Series championship.

The days immediately following her death were filled with callers who came to express sympathy. Instead of receiving mourners in a funeral parlor, Frank opened his home to those who came to share our burden of grief. In many ways it was a curious event. Scenes of weeping in which someone would embrace my brother and pour out sorrow were interspersed with laughter as old friends, long separated, were reunited. A huge pile of sandwiches and refreshments were consumed, and the occasion was like a wake, without booze.

One elderly man, hat held respectfully over his heart with both hands, wandered from place to place, looking for a casket which was not present. His religious tradition included "viewing the remains," and he literally entered every downstairs room of the big old Tudor home, seeking the corpse.

The memorial service which followed a few hours later also contained both tears and laughter. Rich and poor, black and white, young and old attended, for this remarkable woman had paid little attention to life's categories. The presence of so many people who were not social equals testified that the purpose of life is to outlive it.

That evening Frank, the minister-neighbor, the minister's wife, and I went to eat at a nearby restaurant. It had been an exhausting day with emotional peaks and valleys unlike any the four of us had ever experienced. The conversation was muted and restrained as it touched on what had been said and who had been seen that day.

However, as good food worked its restorative powers, the tone of the gathering changed. We began to behave as we had on other occasions when our families had been together. This included the telling of bad jokes, a favorite sport of Frank and myself since childhood. (Editorial Note: Since then my jokes have improved. Frank's have not.) Our friends laughed in the right places, which urged us on.

> Example: Did you hear about the man whose wife ran off with an orangutang?
>
> An orangutang! How awful! Why did she do it?
>
> Who knows? It just goes to show, he shouldn't have married an orangutang in the first place!

Stories and jokes of similar quality were exchanged in rapid order. Our laughter and silliness drew raised eyebrows from nearby patrons.

Suddenly, as if on cue, we all stopped laughing and looked at each other. We were weeping and smiling at the same time. For a moment no words were spoken, but the truth we felt was clear: *all was well*. We knew Ruth was in good hands. We had been behaving as if she were with us still, and, in fact, she was. Nothing for us would ever be the same, particularly for Frank, but we knew God who had brought Ruth to us continued to be with her and with us.

Bernard Shaw, an avowed atheist, once wrote, "Life does not cease to be funny when people die, any more than it ceases to be serious when people laugh." The Christian faith goes one step further. Those who know God is with them even in death also know that death itself is not to be taken too seriously.

The Apostle Paul discovered this in his own way a long time ago:

Who shall separate us from the love of Christ? Shall tribulation, or distress, or persecution, or famine, or nakedness, or peril, or sword. . . .

No, in all these things we are more than conquerors through him who loved us. For I am sure that neither death, nor life, nor angels, nor principalities, nor things present, nor things to come, nor powers, nor height, nor depth, nor anything else in all creation, will be able to separate us from the love of God in Christ Jesus our Lord (Rom. 8:35, 37–39 RSV).

The joke, finally, is on the Grim Reaper.